Social Change through Training and Education

Social Change through Training and Education

HUMAN RELATIONS TIPS FOR EFFECTIVE 21ST CENTURY POLICING

● ● ●

Volume I

Dr. E. Beverly Young

ISBN-13: 9781540661920
ISBN-10: 154066192X

Dedication

Foremost, I dedicate this book to God who gave me His vision for how as an individual I might address the tumultuous relationship existing in some communities between law enforcement officers and the community. I thank Him for using me in the conversation for social change and for answering my prayer to help in any small way possible through the writing, administration and teaching skills He blessed me to have and to use in His service.

Secondly, I dedicate this book to Pastor, Rev. Dr. Charles R. Meile, Jr. and the congregation of the Greater Zion Missionary Baptist Church in Harrisburg, Pennsylvania, with the message that social change is a matter of the heart that only God can and will change.

Next, I dedicate this book to fellow members of the police profession. You (we) made the lifelong commitment to serve the community through impartial and ethical policing practices that assure procedural justice to sustain legitimacy of the profession. I am proud to know you and to have served alongside you.

Finally, I dedicate this book to this generation of lifelong learners who will experience social change through education, new communication and experiences, because they will make social change the reality of the 21st century. In particular, I dedicate this book to Susannah C. Young (niece) and John M. Malone (adopted nephew) asking them to embrace the cause for social change.

John Dewey (1959) wrote, "All that society has accomplished for itself is put through the agency of the school, at the disposal of its future members" (p.34). You are society's future members.

Susannah and John, follow the charge God gave to Joshua. "Strength! Courage! Give it everything you have, heart and soul... Don't get off track, either left or right, so as to make sure you get to where you're going." (Peterson. The Message). Advocate for social change. I challenge you to join in and promote positive and meaningful conversation for social change seeking the will of God each step of the way.

Maybe one day the two of you will co-author a book about social change in America.

Preface

● ● ●

HOW DOES SOCIAL CHANGE INTERSECT with 21st century policing? You can understand or even try to explain the idea of social change using viewpoints framed to explain how humans behave, or how people interact within contexts, or how adults learn over a lifetime. Based on a background as an adult education practitioner and years spent in policing, I define social change through the lens of education and social contexts where life occurs.

The intersection with social change is through the content (channels of communication) within the context (the community, an amalgamation of cultural values) of social engagement. The need and desire to learn fortifies understanding expectations both groups have, motivating people to embrace social change to improve relationships. Dewey (1961) found, "social environment forms the mental and emotional disposition of behavior in individuals by engaging them in activities that arouse and strengthen impulses that have certain purposes and entail certain consequences" (13). [1]

Social change influencing the context of the community and content of communication can be a deliberate or involuntary act if adaptation to new circumstances or change is going to take place (12).[2]

In my series title, I use the terms training and education purposely. The goal of training and education is to change behavior. Training provides individuals with skill adeptness. Education adds to skill by changing a learner's mental and emotional understanding about what they learned and how to apply new knowledge.

Dewey (1961) proposed, "training in distinction from educative teaching" (13).[3] Police training incorporates competencies, academic and legal knowledge aligning with Dewey's proposal for meaningful learning.

Volume 1 in this series, Human Relations Tips for Effective 21st Century Policing, concentrates on the educational ingredient essential for effective and sustainable social change.

Organization of the Book

● ● ●

TRAINING TIPS ARE A LEARNING tool because they are easy to read as quick daily reminders. They provide a non-complex overview of contemporary issues challenging police and law enforcement officers working a myriad of assignments. Tips alert/remind everyone to expectations inherent in the profession and in the position of police/law enforcement officer. Officers vow to serve and protect regardless of the racial makeup, ethnic background, religious beliefs, gender preference or age of the community.

I have been careful to exclude specific reference to police tactics or anything that might compromise officer safety. The content of this book does not replace departmental policy or procedures governing any topic discussed in this book.

I wrote this book for several audiences, police, law enforcement and civilians without police or law enforcement affiliation. Content does not resemble, replicate or replace police academy and in-service instruction.

Chapter 1 begins the discussion. Readers are asked to introspect to determine his/her sustained commitment to policing as a career. Chapter 2 explores communication wellness.

Chapters 3 through seven under a subheading, Community Expectations, comprise information on legitimacy through issues such as differences, ethical decision-making, non-biased based policing, accountability and transparency, as foundation of the police infrastructure and rudimentary to sustaining positive relations between police and residents.

Chapters 8 and 9 speak specifically to policing the community effectively.

Chapter 10 is a review of tips from previous chapters. I take readers back to the basics when understanding the importance of procedural justice to everyone when policing the community. I solicit feedback about procedural justice and the connection with social change, legitimacy, impartial policing and ethical behavior.

Questions to ponder, chapter 11, culminate discussion.

Pages between chapters 1 and 2, 3 and 4 and chapters seven and eight I designed for notetaking.

Contents

Introduction

● ● ●

FIVE CRITICAL BENCHMARKS FOR 21ST century policing are: (1) procedural justice; (2) legitimacy; (3) sustainability; (4) transparency, and (5) ethical behavior. Looking at this list, as a reader you probably ask, what makes these concerns stand out more in the 21st century than in past centuries or since forming police departments.

Numbers may mask underlying problems. Police and law enforcement officers have always been targets for those predisposed to violate the law, sidestep moral and ethical values by disrespecting human life, sometimes at the cost of their own.

The problem entrenched within society has weakened society to the point individuals, through frustration and possibly responding to unfilled promises of change, sometimes respond using protests to send a unified message. Their message, every person's life matters, regardless of age, sex, gender identification, racial and ethnic background, religious following. What is the institutional problem?

In 2014, members of the International Association of Chiefs of Police called a National Summit on Community-Police Relations. On December 18, 2014, President Barack Obama signed Executive Order 13684 creating the President's Task Force on 21st Century Policing. Both efforts were following police confrontations with unarmed African-American males that resulted in death. Participation in the summit and task force meetings included individuals without affiliation to law enforcement. Community leaders, faith-based leaders, representatives from professional organizations participated.

The international association of chiefs of police and the president's task force offered findings in 2015, January and May respectively.

IACP suggested: (1) "to redefine policing in a 21st century democracy; (2) to strength to develop legitimate, sustainable relationships in the community, and (3) implement meaningful ways to define and measure success in community-police relationships as a community" (X). [4]

Members of the task force presented its findings from discussion and interviews using pillars (categories). Pillar 1, building trust, legitimacy, and Pillar 5, training and education, are the flagships for Volume I.

I inferred the institutional problem encompasses human relations addressed individually as the benchmarks for 21st century policing: 1) procedural justice; (2) legitimacy; (3) sustainability; (4) transparency, and (5) ethical behavior.

Part I – Career Fundamentals

● ● ●

Career Success

● ● ●

To Know-to Learn-to Listen-to Lead-
to Receive Correction

OVERVIEW Determining career success requires introspection that examines the reason for selecting a particular profession, to determine continued understanding of the needed commitment to development and using skills, knowledge, and aptitude to achieve a sense of accomplishment, and knowing when the chosen career no longer aligns with a dream.

KEY PRINCIPLES

1. Policing and law enforcement require lifelong **commitment** and affect every area of an officer's life.
2. Never compromising who you are, being willing to learn, having the capacity to listen, leading without prompting, accepting correction are evidence of career accomplishment.
3. Recognizing the need to change and knowing when to change a career requires wisdom.
4. Write your **own** career story; acknowledge that people make mistakes and that the maturing process assists in learning from those mistakes and move on.

Main Discussion Points

Specialists use holistic therapy to restore wholeness to a person using synchronized treatment of each dimension (physical, social, intellectual, spiritual and vocational), using the strength of one dimension to restore balance to another dimension not in sync. To achieve wholeness the doctor carefully identifies and recommends a course of action (plan) that integrates each dimension into the healing process. If unbalance is prevalent in the vocational dimension, eventually the five remaining dimensions will become imbalanced.

For the plan to work, the patient must acknowledge the presence of imbalance and assist with treatment options.

Achieving balance that allows you to **write your own story** begins with introspection (self-analysis) triggered by events or initiated through a self-designed career plan, a career plan that might include asking questions:

- Where do I want to be in five years
- Do I want to become a leader/supervisor
- Do I want to become an instructor
- Has the job changed me
- Do I have a hidden bias preventing me from being relevant in my profession
- Is it time to retire or change professions

After committing to a plan to wholeness,

1. "Pursue excellence
2. **Invest in continuous learning**
3. Make your own breaks
4. **Be relevant to those you serve**
5. Develop courage in the face of adversity" (44-46). [5]

The secret of achievement is to hold a picture of a successful outcome in the mind. (Henry David Thoreau)

NOTES

Interacting with Others-Communication Wellness

● ● ●

OVERVIEW Policing requires interacting with people. The police and the community <u>must</u> interact to achieve understanding. The main method of interacting is talking. Police talk with, answer questions, speak through public meetings, and share information with police from neighboring jurisdictions, talk face-to-face or over the telephone with members of the community.

What happens when police and the community do not want to talk or feel hampered in effectively expressing viewpoints in order to work through differences?

KEY PRINCIPLES

Talking requires listening, hearing, being heard, being understood and understanding other viewpoints.

Interacting integrates an exchange of information between parties with the need to extract information to investigate criminal behavior.

Communicating effectively is a skill. The ability to communicate effectively is an everyday necessity for effective policing. Every police officer is required to communicate verbally and in writing.

Ineffective communication affects officer safety and safety of the community.

What we believe about ourselves may determine how we perceive the importance of interacting or communicating with another person or group of people.

If we believe that we cannot or prefer to avoid having to communicate with people outside our circle of contacts, then we probably do not put forth effort to hone (improve) skills of communicating or interacting with others. Pritchett wrote, "Whether officers realize it or not, their ability to relate to others directly affects every action they perform on duty" (22).[6] Buhler stated likewise, "communication is key in building relationships with others" (19).[7]

a. Effectively policing the community **requires** effective communication. Citizens want to understand clearly, what police are asking. Police want to understand clearly, needs of the community. The community and the police must identify barriers to getting messages heard. What obstructs communicating and interacting within police ranks and within the community?

b. Applicable to police and the community, talking in and of itself is not necessarily communicating. Tracy (2014) stated, "Words account for only 7% of the message, tone of voice accounts for 38%, and body language accounts for 55% of the message" (15).[8] Pritchett (1993) stated correspondingly, "often, nonverbal elements send stronger messages to the listener than verbal ones" (23).[9] The **critical piece** is establishing a bridge between a sender and a receiver making interaction through communication possible. An explicitly valid message relayed through talking and noncontradictory body language is the bridge needed between the sender and the receiver.

Effective communication enhances safety for police and the community.

Part II – Community Expectations

• • •

CHAPTER 3

Differences and Fear

● ● ●

OVERVIEW People fear differences. Some people believe that differences step outside the norm. To explain or mask their lack of understanding, people become fearful, promoting fear and distrust. In response, some people create mental hierarchies equating to granting privilege to some over others. Differences emerge from perception, societal norms, and personal experiences. Fear is not an inherent trait. Fear is a learned behavior. How does one 'unlearn' something?

KEY PRINCIPLES

1. Not all fear is harmful. Fear keeps the human mind alert to concerns for safety, the need to cease destructive behaviors and potential hazard.
2. Fear is an emotional response. Some emotional responses are manageable. Some emotional responses require intervention.
3. Fear is unlearned by actively pursuing understanding.

MAIN DISCUSSION POINTS
**<u>Tips</u> include definitions that help in identifying fear and biases directly influencing a person's ability to perform police tasks effectively and fairly. Keep in mind, these same fears and biases can influence how a

member of the community perceives or interprets behavior displayed by the police.

A. Medical experts define **<u>fear</u>** as an "instinctive response to potential danger".[10] If this is true and inclusive, a reasonable person could believe that <u>every</u> activity, <u>every</u> situation, <u>every</u> individual one encounters in an average day presents potential danger or poses a threat to their well-being, safety, and happiness. Bledsoe and Baskin concluded, "Fear is a complex emotion and can take different shapes and forms in a classroom setting" (36).[11] True or false. Lifelong learning occurs in a classroom setting, unconfined by walls, where you choose to experience or reject opportunities to learn something new about yourself, about others, and about how to overcome and/or cope with every day challenges. Thoughts?

B. Certain fears provide fertile soil for attitudes of prejudice to ripen and proliferate. **Fear** is an emotional response. **Prejudice** is an attitude. Prejudice refers to, "attitudes and beliefs held by an individual or group that inform their decisions and actions" (20).[12]

C. Fear may expose **implicit** (hidden) associations a person makes between the characteristics of an individual and a positive or negative belief or expectation based on stereotypes not based on personal experience. Implicit bias can cause people to pass judgement using gender or race/ethnicity as the sole basis and not on facts of the moment.

D. **Differences** make each person a separate and unique member of society. Unique characteristics distinguishing each person as different include age, gender, race/ethnicity, education, type of work a person performs, skills, health and physical conditions, family structure, etc. Coping mechanisms for managing fear can be experienced through cultural norms a person practices.

E. **Human dimensions** consider the social, emotional, psychological, physical and spiritual parts of a person. No two people think or behave exactly alike and for this reason, developing attitudes that transform into practices of disparate treatment toward another human being can become an outgrowth of fear and implicit bias.

Daily Emphasis

i. To address fear, you must know what makes you fearful.

ii. Assessing fear requires human intervention and response.

iii. Fears can include perception about people, places, and things.

iv. Do not ignore fears and perceptions. Very rarely do fears dissipate during the aging process.

v. Fear can be disabling if you allow it to control your mind and emotional state.

vi. Identifying potential dangers professionally is easier than identifying dangers personally.

vii. Implicit associations disclose a person's belief about someone.

viii. Implicit associations are identifiable using test measures and by examining one's personal motivations.

ix. Implicit associations not fully addressed can obstruct explicit attempts to serve justly.

x. "Implicit bias: the attitudes or stereotypes that affect our understanding, actions and decisions in an unconscious manner" (29).[13]

xi. Acknowledging differences assures a community of procedural justice.

xii. Procedural justice results from impartial treatment, assessment of the facts at the time, and an attitude of service to the community.

xiii. Stereotyping is offensive, limiting when communicating and counter-productive.

xiv. Practicing good policing techniques during police-citizen encounters means assessing each situation individually, based on facts presented at the time, using officer safety to protect the public and the police.

xv. "Individuals who profess egalitarian (democratic) intentions and try to treat all individuals fairly can still unknowingly act in ways that reflect their implicit—***rather than*** explicit—biases" (30).[14]

xvi. Fear can become contagious when people delay identifying cause and effect.

xvii. "…everyday fear can also become debilitating" (33).[15]

xviii. When there is disruption in relationships between the community and police, the potential for increased fear of either stakeholder exists.

xix. Reducing the effects of fear is an active, continuous process.

xx. "Culture too can play an important role in a person's ability to cope with fear" (33).[16]

xxi. Fear can reveal itself through physical, social, physiological, emotional changes and influence decision making.

xxii. Feelings of fear are not criminal. Acting on certain fears may become criminal.

xxiii. Fear presents health risks and consequences for all races and genders regardless of socioeconomic status or place of residence.

xxiv. Since prejudice is an attitude, attitudes are changeable when the willingness to change exists.

xxv. Explicit bias is no less damaging than implicit associations that lead to acts of prejudice.

xxvi. Police officers are not trained to be fearless. Training helps an officer learn to use fear appropriately to identify potential dangers.

xxvii. Training reveals prejudicial attitudes and opportunities to modify behaviors.

xxviii. Differences are challenging; acknowledging differences provide beneficial learning.

xxix. The community looks to police and expects impartial treatment in law enforcement.

xxx. Assessing fear requires human intervention and response. (restated for emphasis)

xxxi. Engaging with the community through problem-solving strategies to reduce crime can help to contradict and reverse negative associations held about people and cultures.

CHAPTER 4

Ethical Decision-making

● ● ●

OVERVIEW The practice of ethical decision-making is a demonstration of the ability to identify appropriate responses that align with values held by an individual or standards set by a department when confronted with temptation and suggestion to react and behave contrary to what is right.

KEY PRINCIPLES

1. Ethical standards are learned behaviors one takes to the job. People do not learn to behave ethically on the job.
2. Behaving ethically fortifies perceptions of legitimacy held by the community about the police and assures an outcome of procedural justice sought by members of the community.
3. Following one's ethical compass guides an officer in making ethical decisions based on doing what is right, not necessarily, what is popular.
4. Lack of trust, bad policing practices, poor police-community relations, corruption are some of many domino effects resulting when an individual chooses to ignore ethical standards.

MAIN DISCUSSION POINTS

Keep in mind, behaving ethically incorporates integrity, values, standards, honesty, virtue, selflessness, courage, character, and honor (13)[17] as rudimentary principles, which a person understands prior to becoming a police officer and must practice while serving in that capacity.

a. **Interferences** in every person's life (without exception) create challenges, making decision making difficult if one does not take a foundation for making ethical decisions to the job. One such interference is witnessing a fellow officer behave unethically. "Ethical conflicts arise when the actions of one person interfere with the interests of another person, group of people, or the <u>community as a whole</u>" (14).[18]

b. **Responses** to ethical dilemmas parallel whom an officer seeks for guidance and the officer's moral knowledge. People use what they already know and then through encouragement from leadership and role models, learn from each circumstance to add to their current level of knowledge. People learn the significance of trust, expectations others have for them, respect, fairness, etc. and use these principles to enhance ethical reasoning when deciding to behave legally or illegally.

c. **Decision-making** is a product of a person's upbringing, teaching received and experiences. ***Whom*** do you rely on to make an ethical decision? ***What*** do you rely on to make that decision? ***How*** do you explain your decision/actions? The answers to these questions and to ethical dilemmas flow from how an individual uses their personal ethical compass as a framework and their understanding of how a response (positive or negative) influences legitimacy in the community.

<u>Legitimacy</u> is "recognition of the right to govern" within a structured joint relationship" (125).[19]

NOTES

CHAPTER 5

Non-Biased Based Policing

● ● ●

OVERVIEW Criminal profilers study and develop suspect summaries based on an analysis of frequency and similarity in behavior patterns, geography, suspect description and forensic evidence in order to detain, pursue, and apprehend suspects. Criminal profiling and racial profiling are dissimilar. Racial profiling or bias-based policing uses race/ethnicity as a primary focus (pretext) to deter criminal behavior proactively or reactively and to gauge suspicion. Using race, ethnicity or religion, and presumption of guilt based on the forenamed descriptors while ignoring other identifiable factors as motivation to stop an individual is bias-based policing or racial profiling.

NON-BIAS BASED POLICE PRACTICES EMPHASIZE pursuing, searching for and/or detaining a person based on reasonable suspicion or probable cause not based solely on the race, ethnicity, or religion of the person.

KEY PRINCIPLES

1. Race-based policing violates civil rights and hinders mobility. Pretext does not validate discretion.

2. The race of the police officer does not minimize the potential for race-based policing to occur.
3. Non-biased policing requires an officer to understand how personal bias when left unchecked, influence the ability to patrol, to practice discretion and to use investigatory tactics equally.
4. **Non-biased policing** promotes legitimacy, ensures procedural justice, strengthens communication with the community, and is an attribute of professionalism. Bias-based policing contradicts the intent of policing and one's oath to serve.

Main Discussion Points
Definitions

1. <u>Race-Based policing or Racial profiling</u>- [*Definition*] "Any action undertaken for reasons of safety, security or public protection that relies on stereotypes...rather than on reasonable suspicion, to single out an individual for greater scrutiny or different treatment" (2).[20]

    [***Teaching point***] An action taken by citizens or police based on inaccurate associations rather than probable cause or reasonable suspicion to believe criminal activity has already occurred or is about to take place, <u>serves to controvert not validate the purpose of policing</u>.
2. <u>Impact factors</u>- [*Definition*] "A person witnessing an event interprets the situation from their frame of reference only. If upon reflection, the only observable factor upon which an action was based appears to be that of color or race then the act is perceived as racial profiling" (8).[21]

    [***Teaching point***] – Perception becomes reality, particularly when members of the community do not understand actions of the police or when the community experiences or witnesses inconsistency in police response for a similar set of circumstances.
3. <u>Implicit</u> [*Definition*] (hidden, preconceived) preferences

4. <u>Explicit bias</u> [*Definition*] are openly expressed behaviors and may combine or bring some hidden prejudices an individual may be unconsciously harboring to the surface.

   [***Teaching point***] - <u>Implicit and explicit biases</u> can surface under certain conditions or stimuli.

Implicit and explicit biases plague everyone and play out daily in our personal and professional interaction with other people.

CHAPTER 6

Sustaining Legitimacy in Policing the Community

● ● ●

OVERVIEW Legitimacy is the <u>belief</u> that discretionary *authority* to control crime and to expect compliance with the law belongs to the police. Because belief exists in the psychological and social dimensions, subject to internal and external influences, beliefs can change. Sustaining legitimacy is an active process.

Key Principles

1. *Legitimacy* is the overarching theme of police discretion, ethical behavior, problem solving and non-biased policing.
2. Legitimacy in policing combines expectation with accountability. It is not an aberration.
3. *Sustaining* legitimacy is a career commitment.

Discussion Points

What is legitimacy?

"<u>Legitimacy</u> refers to judgments ordinary residents make about the authority of the police to make decisions about how to enforce the law and maintain social order. Legitimacy lies within the perceptions of the public ...are subjective, and will vary among jurisdictions" (11). [22]

Police officers make decisions, exercise discretion (a learned behavior), solve problems based on "<u>C</u>ommunity-<u>H</u>arm-<u>E</u>xpectation-<u>E</u>vents-<u>R</u>ecurring and **S**imilarity" (40)[23], and interact with the community without regard for race, ethnicity and religious belief. The public, police leadership, and individual police officers hold the police officer accountable for each action taken and words spoken, without exception.

DOES LEGITIMACY CONTRADICT COMMUNITY-POLICING EFFORTS OR DO THEY WORK IN TANDEM?

Community policing is a patrol strategy with a goal to deter individuals from behaving criminally. Legitimacy is an ideology. A tactic and ideology work in tandem when an ideology becomes the goal and projected outcome of a specific approach. Legitimacy is a projected outcome departments want to realize from instituting an effective community-policing program. Researchers deduce "legitimacy is a property of an authority that leads people to feel that the authority is entitled to be deferred to and obeyed" (514).[24] This means the police profession as an authority has a moral and social obligation to act with equity. Community policing is effective when all stakeholders understand their specific role. Yes, police officers are stakeholders making their role significant.

HOW IS LEGITIMACY SUSTAINED (PROLONGED) AND WHAT DRIVES THE MISSION OF SUSTAINABILITY?

External characteristics of sustainability include the level of communication between parties, whether collaborative efforts are encouraged, and whether cohesive partnerships result. Commitment to recruit, hire, train, supervise and discipline police officers embody some internal characteristics of sustainability. When the community **and** police move forward in the same direction guided by the same vision: the commitment to engage each other through non-confrontational dialogue, to hold each party accountable with an assurance of transparency of non-investigatory information, the vision becomes sustainable to all. Each party channels and considers future changes through continuous dialogue. The commitment to sustainability validates legitimacy of policing the community

Trust, Transparency, Accountability

● ● ●

OVERVIEW Accountability <u>reveals</u> behavior and promotes transparency. Trust is one outcome of transparency. Policing is a transparent profession. The state establishes laws. Municipalities employ individuals to maintain order by enforcing laws. Police officers are accountable to the hiring <u>municipality</u> and take an oath. Police officers are accountable to the <u>community</u> by ensuring procedural justice is the norm of the profession and not an abnormality. Police officers are accountable to <u>themselves</u> to behave fairly and to demonstrate competency. How does an individual officer gauge trust, transparency, and accountability?

Key Principles

1. Exhibiting capability when interacting with a fellow officer or the public, remaining open to training that adds to knowledge and when necessary, corrects behavior to improve performance becomes a symbol of trustworthiness.
2. Being effective in the policing/law enforcement profession means accepting responsibility and being able to articulate the rationale behind decisions.
3. Remaining transparent leads to fairness and competency.

Main Discussion Points

Being able to articulate details, objectively, as an officer promotes transparency and reflects accountability. (**The first gauge**)

Transparency is being able to present a clear view without obstructions, being able to see through something. Transparency does not mean being able to diagnose or explain what drives behavior in all cases. "Transparency is about accounting for your activities, accepting responsibility for them and disclosing fully your performance results, whether good or bad" (46)[25] Barrett states similarly and adds that, "transparency needs to be done in a way that citizens can understand and in a way that allows them to feel that their input is relevant" (56).[26]

Fair treatment demonstrates legitimacy of your actions, allows an officer to use discretion when making decisions on certain infractions, and sends a message of trust to members of the community, even when your actions result in an arrest. (**The second gauge**)

"Trust between law enforcement agencies and the people they protect and serve is essential in a democracy. It is key to the stability of our communities, the integrity of our criminal justice system, and the safe and effective delivery of policing services" (5).[27]

Ethical standards brought to the profession are key to motivating the officer to hold him/herself accountable and to serve the profession in a manner that his/her actions are never less than fair to the community which instills trust in police/law enforcement. (**The third gauge**)

NOTES

Part III - Effective Policing

● ● ●

CHAPTER 8

Community Policing for Today

● ● ●

OVERVIEW Community policing is the practice of interacting with community residents to learn about businesses in the community, the demographics of the community, the needs of the community, and to remain visible and accessible to help solve problems in the community.

Whose job is it to police the community?

Key Principles

1. Building trust
2. Sustaining trust
3. Understanding expectations

Main Discussion Points

1. Policing the community is everybody's business because each individual is a stakeholder in the community.
2. For residents of a community, policing the community means being observant and fully participative when discussing neighborhood problems. It also means policing the attitudes and behavior of residents,

assisting in crime reduction efforts that help to maintain quality of life for all residents.

3. For the individual officer, policing the community means policing his/her own attitude about the profession, expectations of the profession and behavior while on the job within the transparency of the profession.

"Building and maintaining community trust is the cornerstone of successful policing and law enforcement. The building and maintenance of trust takes a great deal of continuous effort" (3).[28]

It is not as difficult as it sounds. Unfortunately, sometime everyone needs a reminder. You sustain trust through consistency and equity. You sustain trust through reflecting on and practicing ethical standards. A police officer sustains trust through his/her willingness to engage.

The question is how to build trust. A police officer builds trust using the same blocks he uses to sustain it; i.e. through consistency, engagement, equity, and ethical behavior.

Residents in a community sustain trust through engagement on the immediate issues affecting quality of life for everyone, equity by not prejudging behavior, and consistency.

Key to finding the missing piece to the puzzle-

"It is important to understand that the <u>complexity</u> of community-police relationships contributes to the unique lens through which each group perceives engagement" (5).[29]

The answer to the opening question - it is everyone's job.

CHAPTER 9

The Actions of One-Community's Perception of All

● ● ●

OVERVIEW When a police officer makes a decision, the decision may shine a spotlight on the officer, the department and the profession regardless of the outcome. A positive or negative decision influences perception in terms of legitimizing policing and can raise concerns about procedural justice for the future.

KEY PRINCIPLES

1. Individual perception can result from personal experiences and/or secondhand knowledge.
2. Perception to some is analogous to traversing a two-lane highway with lanes going in opposite directions. On one side of the highway, members of the community develop a perception of police; on the other side facing another direction, police develop perception about the community.
3. Prejudice and misinformation taint the truthfulness of perception.

MAIN DISCUSSION POINTS

Ideally, people should avoid holding a mental picture comparing perception to traveling on a two-lane highway with each lane facing opposite directions. Unfortunately, there are relationships we might characterize as people pulling in opposite directions with no ending point in sight and without a place to turnaround. What is perception?

Perception explains what a person understands and how he/she understands it. Understanding might be based on what they already know, learn, or experience. Perception is personal awareness.

Without a framework for interpretations, perception can become skewed because written information can be manipulated and what one experiences through visual contact can be tainted by biased or improperly processed individual thought.

Researchers, Rhinerson and Mellen (2016) undertook a study to identify a correlation between length, type, and/or number of interactions with the system on the perception one had of the criminal justice system. The findings they reported confirmed the influence of length, type or number of interactions on perception. In many instances, perception was negative about the system.

How can someone change or influence perception? **Influencing** perception requires personal commitment to performing police tasks impartially and self-assessing motives. **Changing** perception is more difficult. You can only assess your own motives; by attempting to assess another person's motives you become judgmental which leads to the subject of this lesson, the actions of one-community's perception of all. If you can influence another person's opinion because of your profession-centered, impartial approach to performing job tasks, eventually you can change perception of that one person. "Only the parties directly involved can articulate their feelings" (19).[30]

What does this mean to policing a community, safety and decision-making?
The answer is everything.

Part IV - Review

● ● ●

CHAPTER 10

Procedural Justice

● ● ●

OVERVIEW Members of a community expect police officers to serve the profession impartially when patrolling a community, when enforcing laws (state, local and federal) when encountering people of interest for investigation and ultimately to arrest. When all three actions are equal, residents recognize the legitimacy of the police force in their community. As residents acknowledge legitimacy, they also have confidence that procedural justice will be an outcome. The path from practice to procedural justice to legitimacy is neither long nor difficult to walk. How does a police department and its police officers continue to walk that path? Why is it important? Is it difficult or is it easy? YOU decide.

KEY PRINCIPLES

1. Justice is everyone's concern. It is a constitutional right afforded to every member of society, which includes the police.
2. Procedural justice is NOT a new concept. Discussion has resurfaced because of human behavior.
3. Procedural justice is a basic tenet of policing.

MAIN DISCUSSION POINTS

What is procedural justice and how are the elements of its definition applied when discussing social change, legitimacy, impartial policing and ethical behavior?

Overall, residents perceive the legitimacy of policing when they are able to experience, personally or through others, fairness from interactions with the police, impartial treatment during encounters with the police, and if arrested, not being subjected to bias when navigating through the criminal justice system. Procedural justice is the core of their expectation.

The elements of the definition are lengthy; however, they offer a clear understanding of procedural justice. Impartial police practices, the elements of legitimacy and ethical behavior are visible within the definition of procedural justice.

Let us infer that in practice procedural justice means that people want authorities to make decisions based on facts and evidence not bias laced; they want to be treated with respect.

Legitimacy and procedural justice are inseparable principles. When you talk about legitimacy, you cannot neglect addressing the concern for procedural justice.

How does a police department and its police officers walk the path from procedural justice to legitimacy? Consider discussion from earlier chapters.

Ethics are a learned behavior an individual takes to the police profession, not learned through the profession.

(*Chapter 7*) Police officers are accountable to the <u>community</u> by ensuring procedural justice is the norm of the profession and not an anomaly. Police officers are accountable to <u>themselves</u> to behave fairly and to demonstrate competency.

(*Chapter 5*) Perception becomes reality when members of community do not understand actions of the police <u>or when the community experiences or witnesses inconsistency in police response for a similar set of circumstances</u>. Response should be based on the facts presented at the time and in conjunction with concern for safety.

(*Chapter 2*) <u>Effectively</u> policing the community **requires** effective <u>communication</u>. Citizens <u>want</u> to understand clearly, what police are asking. Police <u>want</u> to understand clearly, needs of the community.

CHAPTER 11

Questions to Ponder

• • •

THERE ARE NO RIGHT OR wrong answers to the following questions. Questioning provides opportunity for introspection.

(Chapter 1)
1. Do you still have career enjoyment and are you making a difference in your profession?
2. How has being a police or law enforcement officer changed you personally, psychologically, or emotionally?
3. How frequently do you reassess the decision to become a police or law enforcement officer? What prompts the reassessment?

(Chapter 2)
1. Do you believe you are an effective communicator in all situations? If yes, why?
2. What is <u>one</u> example of how poor communication compromises officer safety?
3. Is this statement logical? "If officer safety becomes compromised, public safety remains unaffected."

(Chapter 4)
1. Think about it. Why is the belief in legitimacy influenced by ethical decision-making?
2. Is it less difficult to make an ethical decision when off the job or on the job?

3. How do you interpret the "*blue code of silence*" in relationship to ethical decision-making?

(Chapter 5)
1. How does racial profiling or race-based policing practices effect officer safety and legitimacy?
2. If you have ever made a pretext stop, what steps did you take to examine your perspective on this practice?
3. Do you personally feel race-based policing or racial profiling is an effective policing strategy to prevent crime?

(Chapter 6)
1. What is a police officer's role in sustaining legitimacy?
2. Does sustained legitimacy threaten officer safety?
3. "If I can articulate my actions based on the circumstances, does that diminish or enhance the department's legitimacy in the community"?

(Chapter 7)
1. Why do people fear transparency?
2. How do you personally assure accountability for your actions?
3. Whom do you seek for trusted advice?

(Chapter 9)
1. Is perception a rush to judgment?

(Chapter 10)
1. Is it difficult or is it easy to walk from practice to procedural justice to legitimacy? Why?

YOU decide!

ENDNOTES

1. John Dewey, *Democracy and Education* (MacMillan Company, New York, 1961), 13.

2. E. Beverly Young, Understanding Social Positioning in the Context of Learning and Participation Experienced by Adult Transitional Residents. (UMI 3396389 (2009), 12.

3. Dewey, *Democracy and Education*, 13.

4. IACP (2015). National Policy Summit on Community-Police Relations: Advancing a Culture of Cohesion and Community Trust. X

5. Richard J. Chambers, "Five Personal Investments for Career Success," *Internal Auditor* (2014):44-46.

6. G.L. Pritchett, "Interpersonal Communication," *FBI Law Enforcement Bulletin* (1993): 22.

7. Patricia Buhler, "Managing in the New Millennium- Six Tips for More Effective Communication," *National Research Bureau* (2009): 19.

8. Brian Tracy, "Getting your Ideas Across," *National Research Bureau* (2014), 15.

9. Pritchett, "Interpersonal Communication," 23.

10. **www.nativeremedies.com**

11. T. Scott Bledsoe and Janice Baskin, "Recognizing Student Fear: The Elephant in the Classroom," *College Teaching* (2014):36.

12. David L. Shields, "Deconstructing the Pyramid of Prejudice," *Phi Delta Kappan* (2014): 20.

13. Cheryl Staats, "Understanding Implicit Bias: What Educators Should Know," *The Education Digest* (2016):29.

14. Staats, "Understanding Implicit Bias," 30.

15. T Scott Bledsoe and Janice J. Baskin, "Recognizing Student Fear: The Elephant in the Classroom," *College Teaching* 62, (2014):33.

16. Bledsoe, "Recognizing Student Fear," 33.

17. Andrew Borrello, "The Power of Police Civility," *FBI Law Enforcement Bulletin* (2012):13.

18. John R. Schaefer, Making Ethical Decisions-A Practical Model," *FBI Law Enforcement Bulletin*, (2002): 14.

19. Anthony Bottoms & Justice Tankebe, "Beyond Procedural Justice," *The Journal of Criminal Law & Criminology* 102, no. 1 (2012):125.

20. Philip Semple, "Profiling and Racial Profiling: An Interactive Exercise," *College Quarterly* (2013): 2.

21. Semple, "Profiling and Racial Profiling," 8.

22. Police Executive Research Forum (PERF). Legitimacy and Procedural Justice: A New Element of Police Leadership. U.S. DOJ-Bureau of Justice Assistance (2014), 11.

23. Ronald V. Clark & John E. Eck, Crime Analysis for Problem Solvers in 60 Small Steps. (USDOJ-Office of Community-Oriented Policing Services, 2005), 40.

24. Jason Sunshine & Tom R. Tyler, "The Role of Procedural Justice and Legitimacy in Shaping Public Support for Policing," *Law and Society Review* (2003): 514.

25. Leigh Johnson, Sustainability-Transparency: Key to Connect with Customers," *The National Provisioner* (2016):46.

26. Katherine Barrett & Richard Greene, "The Trust-Me Factor," *Governing* (2006):56.

27. Final Report of the President's Task Force on 21st Century Policing, 2015. 5.

28. IACP and USDOJ.2009. 3.

29. IACP National Summit.2015. 5.

30. Wayne A. Jones. Racial Profiling: Balancing Safety with Citizens' Rights. (Diverse Issues in Higher Education, 2014) 19.

BIBLIOGRAPHY

Alba, Richard, Ruben G. Rumbaut, and Karen Marotz. "A Distorted Nation: Perceptions of Racial/Ethnic Group Sizes and Attitudes Toward Immigrants and Other Minorities." *Social Forces* 84, no. 2 (2005).

Barrett, Katherine, and Richard Greene. "The Trust-Me Factor." *Governing*, 2006, 56-59.

Bledsoe, T Scott, and Janice J. Baskin. "Recognizing Student Fear: The Elephant in the Classroom." *College Teaching* 62 (2014), 32-41.

Borrello, Andrew. "The Power of Police Civility." *FBI Law Enforcement Bulletin*, 2012, 13-15.

Bottoms, Anthony, and Justice Tankebe. "Beyond Procedural Justice." *The Journal of Criminal Law & Criminology* 102, no. 1 (2012), 119-170.

Buhler, Patricia M. "Managing in the New Millennium - Six Tips for More Productive Communication." *National Research Bureau*, 2009, 19-21.

Chambers, Richard. "Five Personal Investments for Career Success." *Internal Auditor*, 2014, 43-46.

Clarke, Ronald V., and John E. Eck. *Crime Analysis for Problem Solvers in 60 Small Steps*. US DOJ-Office of Community-Oriented Policing Services, 2005.

Dewey, John. "Education as a Social Function." In *Democracy and Education*, 10-22. New York: MacMillan Company, 1961.

Dunn, Ronnie A. "Racial Profiling: A Persistent Civil Rights Challenge even in the 21st Century." *Case Western Reserve Law Review* 66, no. 4 (2016), 957-992.

Dworkin, Martin S., editor. *Dewey on Education Selections*. New York: Teachers College, Columbia University, 1959.

Edelman, Perry, and Jon Montague. "Whole-Person Wellness." *Long Term Living*, 2008, 20-25.

Executive Order 13684. Establishment of the President's Task Force on 21st Century Policing. Federal Register. 79 (246), 2014.

Final Report of the President's Task Force on 21st Century Policing. 2015.

Fitch, Brian D. "Focus on Ethics-Rethinking Ethics in Law Enforcement." *FBI Law Enforcement Bulletin*, 2011, 18-24.

Greenlee, Craig T. "Safety Zone - Issues Surrounding Policing on Campus Raise Questions about Security and Profiling." *The Chronicle of Higher Education - Diverse Issues in Higher Education*, 2016, 17-21.

International Association of Chiefs of Police. *Building Trust between the Police and the Citizens they Serve" An Internal Affairs Promising Practices Guide for Local Law Enforcement*. Office of Community-Oriented Policing Services, U.S. Department of Justice, 2009.

International Association of Chiefs of Police. *National Policy Summit on Community-Police Relations: Advancing a Culture of Cohesion and Community Trust*. IACP, 2015. http://www.theiacp.org/.. CommunityPoliceRelationsSummitReport_Jan15.pdf.

Johnson, Leigh A. "Sustainability-Transparency: Key to Connect with Customers." *The National Provisioner*, 2016, 46-48.

Jones, Dan. "Much Ado About Fighting." *New Scientist* 215, no. 2883 (2012).

Peterson, Eugene H. "The Message." Last modified 2002. https://www.bible-gateway.com/passage/?search=Joshua+1:7&version=MSG.

Police Executive Research Forum. "Legitimacy and Procedural Justice: A New Element of Police Leadership." Last modified 2014. http://www.policeforum.org/assets/docs/Free_Online_Documents/Leadership...

Pritchett, Garry L. "Interpersonal Communication." *FBI Law Enforcement Bulletin* 62, no. 7 (1993), 22-27.

Rhinerson, Samantha, and Ronald Mellen. "Perceptions of the Criminal Justice System." *American Jails*, 2016, 33-36.

Schafer, John R. "Making Ethical Decisions-A Practical Model." *FBI Law Enforcement Bulletin*, 2002, 14-18.

Semple, Philip. "Profiling and Racial Profiling: An Interactive Exercise." *College Quarterly* 16, no. 4 (2013).

Shields, David L. "Deconstructing the Pyramid of Prejudice." *Phi Delta Kappan* 96, no. 6 (2014), 20-25.

Staats, Cheryl. "Understanding Implicit Bias: What Educators Should Know." *The Education Digest*, 2016, 29-39.

Sunshine, Jason, and Tom R. Tyler. "The Role of Procedural Justice and Legitimacy in Shaping Public Support for Policing." *Law and Society Review* 37, no. 3 (2003), 513-547.

Tracy, Brian. "Getting Your Ideas Across." *National Research Bureau*, 2014, 14-16.

Weitzer, Ronald, and Steven A. Tuch. "Race and Perceptions of Police Misconduct." *Social Problems* 51, no. 3 (2004).

Young, E Beverly. "Understanding Social Positioning in the Context of Learning and Participation Experienced by Adult Transitional Residents." PhD diss., Walden University, 2010. ProQuest (3396389).

ABOUT THE AUTHOR

I am Dr. E. Beverly Young, Adult Learning Strategies Consultant, who specializes in developing curriculum for Police and Law Enforcement training and Instructor Development.

My experience includes Course Content reviews, public speaking, and serving on Critical Incident Review Panels, Police Hiring and Promotional Review Boards.

Career milestones providing the strong foundation for these services include numerous years of service as a municipal police officer and commander, Pennsylvania Act 120 certified. (Act 120 is the Municipal Police Education and Training Act of Pennsylvania.) Additional experience includes police instructor certification, teaching in-service and professional development classes, overseeing compliance with certification and training standards, reviewing course content, mentoring, adjunct faculty teaching and advisory board membership.

I am a native of Brooklyn, New York, youngest of two children, graduate of Walden and Temple Universities, founder and executive director of EbevyYG Learning Solutions, LLC. Learning Solutions is a company with a business plan to offer curriculum development services for Police and Law Enforcement classes that introduce learners to the connection of research and contemporary practices relating to 21st century policing issues.

Currently, I am one of two project team leaders rewriting the academy curriculum for the Massachusetts Police Training Commission. Additionally, I am a part of a project team hired to review police-community relations policies and practices to improve community interaction for a police department in Pennsylvania.

During 2016, the Learning Solutions Team was one of nine teams considered and interviewed by the U.S. Department of Justice and residents of Ferguson, Missouri to monitor implementation of the Consent Decree settled on with Ferguson.

I hope information in Volume I of the Social Change through Training & Education series has helped to clarify some issues that we as a <u>community</u> must address to heal the fractured relationship between police and the community. Training and education provide the physical therapy needed to bring understanding and change.

Feel free to contact me through email, **ebevyyg@solution4u.com**. Notification of the release of future volumes in this series will be posted on my website (**www.ebevyyg-learningsolutions.com**).

Grace and Mercy get me up in the morning. Hope eases the wait. Faith keeps me steadfast.

To God be the glory for the things He has done!
E *Bev* Doc

www.ingramcontent.com/pod-product-compliance
Lightning Source LLC
Chambersburg PA
CBHW071330310526
45789CB00017B/2155